Original title:
Odes to Orbital Oddities

Copyright © 2025 Creative Arts Management OÜ
All rights reserved.

Author: Dexter Sullivan
ISBN HARDBACK: 978-1-80567-843-4
ISBN PAPERBACK: 978-1-80567-964-6

A Journey through Cosmic Kaleidoscopes

In a vacuum where cats play,
Chasing stardust every day,
Galactic mice do run and hide,
On flying tacos, they take pride.

Planets wobble, dance a jig,
While comets twirl, let's not be big,
A donut star rolls through the night,
Its sprinkles sparkling, what a sight!

Asteroids wear silly hats,
As rocket ships chat with the bats,
A starfish swims through cosmic soup,
As alien frogs do the loop-de-loop.

In this twisty cosmic game,
Nothing ever is the same,
Join the ride, just hold on tight,
Through kaleidoscopes of pure delight.

The Elysium of Uncharted Skies

A cloud made of candy rains down gum,
While mushrooms dance with a silly thrum,
Sailing ships with wings of cheese,
Tugging at dreams with a gentle breeze.

The moons play hopscotch, laughing bold,
In a realm where tales are spun and told,
Saturn's rings are a jump rope craze,
Swinging clowns in bright, whirly ways.

Jellyfish float through cosmic beams,
While space whales sing whimsical dreams,
Marshmallow meteors bounce around,
In this joyous, uncharted ground.

So grab your broom and sweep the stars,
Paint the night with celery jars,
In this funny sky, come take a ride,
To the universe's silly side.

Harmonizing with the Cosmos' Rhythm

In a galaxy spinning, a dance so free,
Aliens tap-dancing on comets, you see.
Planets clap a beat, asteroids roll,
Singing with joy, it's a cosmic stroll.

Stars in the night swirl, a shimmering show,
Gravity's pulling, but they're stealing the glow.
With giggles from nebulae, laughter takes flight,
Outer space parties go on every night.

Fantasies of the Far-Reaching Universe

Zebras ride moons, dreaming quite grand,
While asteroids juggle in a jovial band.
Black holes play peekaboo, swirling around,
Comets are skateboards that soar from the ground.

Planets dressed up in their jewelry bright,
Dance under starlight, how charming a sight!
Galactic pranks happen behind cosmic doors,
With laughter echoing from space's vast shores.

The Symphony of Galactic Fragments

A meteor shower with a drumroll loud,
Space critters jiving, all gleeful and proud.
Satellites sing harmony, tuning their strings,
A symphonic mess that the universe brings.

Dust bunnies whirl in a wacky ballet,
While quasars whisper secrets of play.
Celestial giggles from afar, so unique,
Echo through voids, tickling stars on the cheek.

Chasing Starlight's Embrace

Fleeting beams of light, tickle and tease,
With fireflies in space, dancing with ease.
Galactic marathons in the void's embrace,
Racing with comets, what a wild chase!

Wormholes with jokes that never grow old,
As asteroids tell tales that sparkle like gold.
In the cosmic circus, there's fun every day,
Chasing starlight's glimmer, come join the play!

Choreography of Celestial Bodies

Planets waltz in twinkling dance,
Stars trip over their own expanse.
Comets giggle, swishing by,
While moons play tag and bounce on high.

Asteroids are clumsy, what a sight,
Bumping into friends in their flight.
Gas giants puff, pretending grace,
But lose their cool in cosmic space.

Cosmic Echoes in Deep Space

In the vastness, sounds go 'whoosh',
Neptune is a bassoon, oh what a push!
Saturn's rings jingle, such sweet noise,
Even black holes emit strange joys.

'Clap your hands!' the stars all say,
Echoes ripple, bouncing away.
Planets laugh, they can't resist,
As lightyears giggle, a cosmic twist.

The Gravity of Oddball Worlds

Here comes a planet, feeling low,
With gravity that's way too slow.
It tries to jump but just can't soar,
And ends up flat, braving the floor.

A whimsical moon wears hats with glee,
Spinning around like a jubilee.
Strange orbits lead to silly sights,
Zany worlds on wild cosmic flights.

Tapestry of the Hidden Constellations

In the dark, a cat finds a star,
Mismatched patterns, oh how bizarre!
A fish debates with a dancing chair,
While a sock wonders if it's rare.

These constellations twinkle and tease,
With shapes that only cosmic folks see.
They giggle in light-years and twine,
Wrapped in humor, forever divine.

Reflections in a Cosmic Pond

In a pond of starlight, frogs leap high,
Catching comets as they fly by.
They croak out melodies of pure delight,
As meteors giggle in the night.

Ripples expand with a splashy flair,
Aliens dance without a care.
Toads wear helmets, hopping with glee,
Waving to space whales that glide past tree.

Lunar lilies bloom and sway,
While asteroid ducks frolic and play.
In this cosmic puddle, laughter reigns,
Jokes about black holes fill the veins.

A giggling sun spins around,
Tickling planets with a joyful sound.
In this whimsical pond, all is bright,
Where every star shines, a comedic light.

Love Among the Astral Phenomena

A comet and a star went on a date,
Sharing pizza on their cosmic plate.
With each slice, they laughed in the void,
Over ridiculous moons they had toyed.

The asteroids winked, feeling the vibe,
Shooting for love through the cosmic tribe.
With every twinkle and shimmer they'd find,
A celestial bond, beautifully blind.

Dancing on rings of pastel delight,
While Saturn spun tales under the light.
Magnetic fields pulled them ever near,
Whispered secrets only they could hear.

As galaxies twirled in a cosmic show,
Love brewed gently where stardust flows.
Their hearts collided, a bashful spark,
In the dark expanse, they hit the mark.

The Mythos of the Orbiting Anomalies

In a realm where logic loves to bend,
Planets argue, claiming to be friends.
Anomalies prance, defying all rules,
Chasing each other like playful fools.

Gravity grumbles in sarcastic tones,
While comets berate their wobbling bones.
A moon trips over its own tired craters,
As space-time folds, it rebels like skaters.

Each tale feels absurd, as gravity shakes,
Stars calling out for the next great breaks.
With loops and spins, the narratives churn,
In a universe where oddities burn.

Yet amidst the chaos, laughter does sail,
As black holes open, we chuckle and pale.
Orbiting logic finds no escape,
In this merry mess, all shapes take shape.

Chants from the Celestial Void

In the void where whispers begin to play,
Galactic giggles echo, night turns to day.
Stars hum tunes in an offbeat jam,
While dark matter sways, a cosmic sham.

Nebulas twirl in colors so bold,
While time warps around them, stories unfold.
Pulsars shout jokes in a strobe-light dance,
As planets pirouette, lost in romance.

Echoes of laughter bounce off the stars,
Comedic cracks travel from Venus to Mars.
The black holes chuckle, a mysterious glee,
As they swallow laughter, endlessly free.

So join the chorus of the celestial sound,
In this quirky universe, joy knows no bound.
With each strange chant, let confusion dissipate,
As we laugh at the cosmos—oh, isn't it great?

Wanderlust Among the Asteroids

Asteroids dance in a cosmic jig,
With rocks in tow, they all dig.
A tumble here, a bounce there,
Who knew space could be so rare?

Zipping past in a sunlit race,
They wear their craters with such grace.
Do they laugh, do they sigh?
Floating by, oh my, oh my!

Caught in their rocky embrace,
It's a chaotic, merry place.
A madcap ball of cosmic lore,
Who needs a disco when you can explore?

Whirling and twirling, they play,
Just dodging gravity's heavy sway.
Oh, space rocks, what a sight!
In your wobbly dance of delight!

Echoes of Forgotten Planets

Once great worlds, now a whisper,
Their glory faded, became a drifter.
In the silence, tales unfold,
Of giants in hues of blue and gold.

Old Jupiter's skirts are flaring,
While Pluto lounges, non-caring.
"Hey, remember me?" he shouts,
But all they hear are cosmic doubts.

Lost in the void, stars giggle,
Silent laughter makes them wiggle.
What mischief did they dare?
A history lost in stellar air!

Resurrected in daydreams bright,
These planets dance, oh, what a sight!
With every spin, they claim their fame,
In the vastness, it's all just the same!

The Lure of Wandering Comets

Comets chase in a vibrant play,
Their fuzzy tails lead the way.
"Catch me if you can!" they tease,
While stardust floats like a cool breeze.

Through the dark, they swerve and glide,
A cosmic ship on a joyride.
Whipping past each starry friend,
With laughter that seems to never end.

In their trails, dreams spark and glow,
Sprinting towards the next star-show.
Do they know where they'll land?
Or just wing it, like a band?

Oh comet, you merry traveler bold,
With tales of wonders yet to be told.
In the night sky, you steal the stage,
An interstellar dance, a cosmic page!

Revelations from the Rings of Saturn

Saturn spins in rings of glee,
Stripes of color, wild and free.
Little moons waltz round the dance,
In celestial skirts, they take a chance.

"Hey, what's that?" a passerby calls,
As a moon falls into space brawls.
"Oh don't worry, we're just jesting,
Just orbital tomfoolery, no resting!"

The ice and rock twirl in tune,
As if the stars were a merry cartoon.
Glimmering bright, their secrets unfold,
In orbits of laughter, tales manifold.

With each spin, revelations arise,
Shiny treasures light up the skies.
Oh Saturn, what a playful spree,
You make the cosmos a grand jubilee!

The Alchemy of Celestial Bittersweet

In a garden where comets bloom,
Rockets trade jokes with the moon.
Stars wear hats made of cheese,
While planets dance in a cosmic breeze.

Jupiter spills its fizzy soda,
While Mars wears a bright pink moda.
Saturn juggles its rings with flair,
As black holes laugh without a care.

Neptune sings in tones so high,
As dandelion seeds drift by.
The universe cracks jokes 'til dawn,
With goofy aliens all around to yawn.

Galaxies collide in a funny fight,
While suns glow brightly, oh what a sight!
They chase their tails around the void,
In this quirky dance, none's annoyed.

Epitaph for an Alien World

Here lies a planet known for its pies,
Where the inhabitants hatch surprise flies.
With tentacles flailing and eyes so wide,
They served soup made from a moonlit tide.

Once, they hosted a dance of the stars,
And each one arrived in old rusty cars.
But when gravity took a nap one night,
They floated up high, what a fright!

The alien king lost his crown of gold,
To a rogue asteroid so brave, yet bold.
Now the world spins in joyous glee,
With laughter echoing from sea to sea.

So raise a toast with fizzy drink,
To the odd beings that make us think!
In their quirky realm, forever they'll stay,
Making us chuckle in their own way.

Harmony in Orbital Disarray

In the orbits of laughter, they spin around,
Chaos and joy in their cosmic sound.
Venus sings off-key, just for the fun,
While Earth groans loudly; 'Oh, not this one!'

Uranus rolls over, in a fit of giggles,
As meteors play hide and seek with wiggles.
Each asteroid blushes with every tease,
In this fun-filled cosmos, they do as they please.

Life here is silly, with no sense of time,
Comets tap dance in a rhythmical rhyme.
Neptune plays drums crafted from ice,
While Pluto joins in, not thinking twice.

So embrace the mayhem, let's all take flight,
In this zany galaxy, feels so right.
With laughter and chaos, we twist and sway,
In harmony, we'll dance the night away.

The Soliloquy of the Spinning Orbs

Oh, to be a planet, round and stout,
Spinning slowly, what's that about?
Do I make faces at stars up high?
Or twirl in my loneliness, oh my!?

When the moon winks with a playful glance,
I offer a jig in this cosmic dance.
Saturn's rings are the sparkly guise,
That hide my vibrant, blushing skies.

Mars shoots glitter with a laser beam,
While I lasso meteors, it's quite the dream.
With stars as my audience, I stand and spin,
Mumbling for company, my metal skin.

In this vastness, I seek a friend,
To twirl and laugh until the end.
So here's to the whims of the night so dark,
Let's dance in the glow of our silly spark.

Celestial Whispers of the Unknown

In the vastness where comets sail,
A pizza slice on a cosmic trail.
Planets wobble in silly glee,
Who knew space could be so free?

Asteroids dance with a caffeinated flair,
While quasars gossip without a care.
Aliens chuckle on their way to Mars,
Sending memes on falling stars.

Rockets giggle as they zoom and glide,
Juggling moons like they're on a ride.
Galaxies spin in a swirl of fun,
Singing songs 'til the day is done.

Dancing with Distant Satellites

Satellites twirl like they're at a ball,
Spin and whirl, ready to fall.
They take selfies with the Sun so bright,
Flashing smiles in the deep of night.

With every orbit, a cosmic tease,
Gravity pulls, but they dance with ease.
In orbits entangled, they sway and spin,
To a quirky tune that makes them grin.

A waltz with planets is all the rage,
As black holes twerk on a galactic stage.
The Milky Way hums a tune that's catchy,
Even space dust finds it too scratchy!

The Gravity of Dreams

A dreamer floats on a cloud of hype,
While gravity teases with its slippery type.
Stars bounce like children, carefree and wild,
In a universe that feels like a child.

With every thought, worlds stretch and bend,
The laws of physics decide to pretend.
Astro-nuts giggle, flipping through space,
Making jokes in the intergalactic race.

Eclipses play peekaboo, slyly, oh my!
Filling the cosmos with laughter and sigh.
Stardust dances, creating a scene,
Where nightmares vanish, and fun is routine.

Reflections on a Cosmic Mosaic

In cosmic mirrors, worlds collide,
With splashes of colors, they take a ride.
Nebulas giggle in pastel hues,
While supernovae offer dazzling views.

Planets prance in their glittery coats,
With rings that twirl like playful boats.
They sing a chorus of misplaced socks,
Mismatched in orbit, ticking like clocks.

Black holes plot while stars light the night,
Creating a canvas, a joyful sight.
In the grand scheme, it's all a delight,
A prism of laughter, shining so bright.

Interstellar Adrift in the Night

A spaceship lost its way, quite silly,
Floating past a comet, feeling frilly.
Stars wink and giggle, what a sight!
Twirling through the darkness, oh what a night!

The captain's snack, a floating pie,
Drifting slowly, oh my, oh my!
Planets peek from behind their veils,
Whispering secrets in cosmic tales.

Asteroids dance in the shimmering space,
Bots trying to keep up, oh, what a race!
With each twist and turn, they float and glide,
In a cosmic game of tag, full of pride.

A flicker of hope in the stellar mess,
Finding giggles in the cosmic chess.
In the vastness, we're never alone,
Just space-faring friends, like gnomes on loan!

Portraits of Planets, Painted in Light

Mars wore a red coat, quite prim and neat,
While Venus primps in her sparkly sheet.
Jupiter struts, a king with his crown,
Swaying like he owns the whole town!

Saturn spins rings like a fashion show,
Pluto's left out, but still puts on a glow.
Earth grins broadly, a cheeky delight,
With a wink at the cosmos, shining bright!

Neptune holds a party in shades of blue,
While Uranus giggles, what a view!
The stars paint smiles, twinkling away,
In a gallery of giggles where planets play.

In the cosmic studio where art takes flight,
Every planet shines, a marvelous sight!
Hilarity reigns in the vastness above,
A tapestry woven with laughter and love!

The Lament of a Lost Galaxy

In a nebula's hug, I found my way,
But now I'm lost, oh woe, I must say!
Stars are chuckling, playing hide-and-seek,
While I float around, feeling quite meek.

"Where's the Milky Way?" I loudly cry,
Comets shoot by with a wink and a sigh.
Galaxies twirl, lost in their dance,
While I'm just here, wishing for a glance.

Black holes snicker, "You'll never get out!"
But I'm made for the cosmos, without a doubt.
Evading the edge of the cosmic blight,
Where's my GPS in this immense night?

But through all the panic and silly dismay,
I'll twirl with the stars and drift in the fray.
For even lost in a vast, swirling scene,
I'll sprinkle some laughter in spaces unseen!

A Tapestry of Celestial Whimsy

The sun plays tag with the flying moon,
Chasing shadows while humming a tune.
Galaxies giggle in spiraled delight,
Painting the cosmos with beams of light.

Shooting stars tumble, with wishes to spare,
While comets throw pies in the galactic air.
Venus twirls wildly in her glittery dress,
While Martians cheer on, feeling quite blessed.

Asteroids hop like froggies in fall,
Planetary pranks in the cosmic ball.
Saturn's rings jingle as they sway,
In this wondrous theater, the stars come to play!

So gather 'round, you cosmic crew,
Join in the fun, there's much to pursue!
For in this universe, funny things loom,
Creating smiles that forever bloom!

Sonnet for a Wandering Comet

A comet drifts with a tail so bright,
It wags like a puppy, oh what a sight!
Chasing its dreams past the stars and dust,
Leaving behind a trail—it's a must!

Nibbling on meteorites for a snack,
This stellar wanderer won't turn back.
It chuckles as planets glare and pout,
'Catch me if you can!' it shouts out loud.

With each zippy pass, it grins and sway,
Joking with asteroids, 'Come on, let's play!'
A dance in the void where laughter is free,
A ballet of chaos, oh can't you see?

So raise a toast to this traveler bold,
A celestial jester with tales to unfold!

Ballad of the Cosmic Strangers

In the night sky, so vast and wide,
Stranded stars throw a cosmic ride.
'Where are we going?' they ask with glee,
'Just follow me; you'll see, you'll see!'

One star is lost, but never alone,
With a rogue planet and a moon of stone.
They tell silly jokes, and a few bad puns,
A trio of misfits having good runs.

Galaxies twinkle, join in the fun,
'Why did the comet get lost on the run?'
They laugh so hard at their silly plight,
As light-years melt into pure delight.

Through orbits and rings, they'll wander on,
These cosmic strangers from dusk till dawn.

Serenade Beneath the Cosmic Veil

Under a blanket of shimmering stars,
A dance takes place with the strange guitar.
Planets twirl slowly, missing a beat,
While the moons chuckle softly, tapping their feet.

'Hey there, Venus, do you know this tune?'
'Oh, it's a bop that I heard from the moon!'
'Let's swipe to the left on an asteroid's groove,
And see if we can't find our cosmic move!'

Neptune spins wildly, offers a whirl,
Saturn just laughs, rings in a twirl.
The sun beams down, a spotlight so warm,
As stars all join in, creating the form.

In this grand ballet, no stakes cause strife,
Just a musical swirl that's full of life.

Lament of the Lost Satellites

Oh, satellites lost in the deep, dark space,
Once so bright, now a ghostly trace.
They reminisce on orbits once proud,
Singing their woes to the drifting cloud.

'Remember when we buzzed that planet's heat?
Now we float aimless with nothing to greet.'
They chuckle through static, their voices a buzz,
'At least we're still here, whatever that was!'

An echo from Mars offers a grin,
'Lost pals, you're late for the galactic spin!'
With jests and jabs, they'll chart their own fate,
Making the most of their cosmic state.

So dance, you lost souls, in the deep of night,
While you twinkle away, oh what a sight!

Cosmic Ballads in the Void

In the deep of space, where lost socks roam,
Asteroids waltz, calling the stars home.
Comets with tails that tickle the moon,
Dance with the planets, all in a tune.

Saturn's rings sparkle, a giant hula hoop,
While Mars joins the party, making a whoop!
Jupiter's stormy, but still takes a spin,
In this cosmic circus, let the laughs begin.

Neptune blows bubbles, a playful blast,
While Venus plays peek-a-boo, liftoff so fast.
Galaxies giggle, swirling in jest,
In a universe vast, we all are blessed.

So let's all embrace this galactic jest,
Life on a comet? A celestial fest!
With every twinkle, we'll share a laugh,
In our orbit of wonders, let joy be the path.

Celestial Thoughts on a Spinning Axis

Earth spins and twirls, it's quite in a rush,
Like a cat chasing lights, all in a hush.
Oh, the gravity dips when you leap in surprise,
As moonbeams play tag, dodging glimmering skies.

Mercury zips past, a speedster, it's true,
While Venus throws shade, in a bright evening hue.
There's laughter in darkness, a stellar parade,
As we twirl on this axis, our worries will fade.

Asteroids giggle, as they bounce through the night,
With all galaxies laughing, what a glorious sight!
Red giants wink slowly, glowing with joy,
In the whirl of the cosmos, no care to destroy.

So join this spin, let's twirl round the sun,
With laughter and light, it's a cosmic run.
A frolic in starlight, let's dance on a whim,
In this cosmic ballet, our laughter won't dim.

Harmonies of Light and Shadow

Stars sing in whispers, shadows take flight,
Galactic giggles echo deep in the night.
A black hole hiccups, swallowing dreams,
While nebulae bloom in ridiculous themes.

Lightyears are silly, they stretch out so far,
But not as absurd as a dancing quasar!
Pulsars keep time like a cosmic drumbeat,
While space dust does cartwheels, a treat oh so sweet.

Eclipses with masks, having fun on their days,
Leave planets in stitches, in starlit arrays.
Astro-antics abound in the shimmering glow,
Of twinkling celestial, strike a pose, strike a show!

So raise your glass high, to the cosmic dance,
In this grand universe, let's leap at a chance.
For laughter's the light, that will guide our way,
In harmonies bright, let's frolic and sway.

The Silhouettes of Orbiting Dreams

Shadows of planets cast in moonbeams,
Whispering tales of orbiting dreams.
Galaxies gossip, their twinkling glow,
Sharing sweet secrets that nobody knows.

Oort clouds with laughter, floating about,
Singing of comets with tails that shout.
Uranus has jokes that'll spin you around,
As Neptune chuckles, a celestial sound.

Rings of Saturn giggle in shimmering spins,
While shooting stars race, sharing dreams like twins.
A cosmic delight in a whimsical scene,
Where shadows of starlight make every heart keen.

So let's share a chuckle, let's orbit and fly,
In this universe vast, we'll reach for the sky.
With every rotation, find joy in the scheme,
In the silhouettes bright, we chase every dream.

When Moons Collide with Memory

In a dance of awkward grace,
Two moons forgot their place.
They twirled and bumped, they spun,
In a cosmic game of run.

Asteroids laughed, they took a peek,
At the two moons playing hide and seek.
With a giggle, they rolled on by,
While comets wondering, "Oh my!"

One moon said, "Do you remember,
The time we lit up December?"
The other, puzzled, scratched its face,
"Was that before or after space?"

But with every twist and twirl,
They created a celestial swirl.
In their chaos, they found a rhyme,
Time is funny in orbit's climb.

Stellar Chronicles of the Past

In the pages of the night,
Stars giggle with delight.
"Remember when we made that mess?
All those wishes, what a stress!"

Once a black hole tried to grin,
But it sucked its laughter in.
"Can dark matter really appreciate?
Or is it always late for fate?"

Planets shared their timeless tales,
Of alien friends and crazy gales.
"Oh, the time we lost our rings,
And danced like we were minstrels' kings!"

And as the universe spins along,
These stars compose their silly song.
In a cosmos full of glee,
Memories are where we all agree.

The Enigmas of Deep Space

Out in the void where mysteries creep,
Planets are giggling and hardly sleep.
"What's the meaning of a comet's tail?
Is it just a long, fuzzy trail?"

Galaxies whisper their secrets low,
As black holes chat about their best show.
"Did you hear about the star who shined?
It went supernova, lost its mind!"

Zany quasars race past,
In their antics, they drift so fast.
With a wiggle and a flip, they tease,
Space isn't serious, it aims to please!

So if you seek what's out there wide,
Join the cosmic silliness, become a guide.
In the enigmas of deep space, you'll find,
Laughter lingers and sparkles unwind.

Fragments of Stardust and Time

Once a piece of stardust said,
"I look like I have a crown on my head!"
The comet replied with a sparkle bright,
"Tell me about it, I'm swishing tonight!"

Time giggled like a child in the breeze,
"Don't mind me, I'm just here to tease!"
"Let's race the planets, what do you say?
After all, what's the limit of a day?"

Meteors crashed in dashes of sass,
Shouting, "Time flies when you're having class!"
But as they tumbled past the stars,
They realized, it's all just who we are!

In the fragments, joy intertwines,
With the universe full of playful designs.
So dance with a smile at all you see,
For laughter in space is truly free!

The Odyssey of Astral Ambiguities

In cosmic realms where comets creep,
Stars giggle softly, lost in deep,
Aliens toast with stardust wine,
While planets shuffle, so benign.

Meteors wear silly, shining hats,
Orbiting dogs chase after chats,
Galaxies spin in wobbly cheer,
As black holes whisper, 'Come in here!'

A moonbeam hiccups, lands askew,
And Saturn's rings play peekaboo,
Constellations argue who is best,
While starlight sparkles, fully dressed.

In this vast dance of nightly cheer,
Cosmic oddballs gather here,
With laughter echoing in the skies,
The universe winks with twinkling eyes.

The Dance of the Binary Stars

Two stars pirouette, spinning bright,
Chasing shadows in the night,
With laughter echoing from afar,
They twirl and leap, a dazzling star.

One wears a tutu, sparkly and bold,
The other dons a cape, a sight to behold,
They bump and jive in their stellar waltz,
Making meteors giggle, they halt.

Neighbors peek from their celestial homes,
Wondering how to join these poems,
Trail of laughter fills the void,
As space itself feels joyous and buoyed.

In this bizarre, celestial play,
Stars dance and wiggle, night to day,
With harmony crafted in cosmic glee,
The universe teases, 'Come dance with me!'

Capture of the Celestial Mirage

Chasing shadows across the sky,
A mirage laughs, 'Oh, give it a try!'
Planets scramble, make a fuss,
Who knew space could have such a plus?

A comet sneezes, sending sparkles wide,
While an asteroid tries a wild ride,
With glittering trails and trails of dust,
The cosmic dreamers must adjust.

Despite the chaos, they keep their cool,
Waltzing around like stars in school,
Eager to snag the glowing light,
A mirage giggles, 'Not tonight!'

Endless laughter rings through the void,
Where dreams of space simply can't be toyed,
In this surreal, cosmic charade,
Happiness flows in vast cascade.

Glimpses of the Galactic Outsiders

Outside the norm, the quirky dwell,
With tales to share and jokes to tell,
A triangle star with a puppet show,
Invites the planets to come and glow.

Caffeine comets whisk around the Sun,
Spilling coffee beans, oh what fun!
An alien tunes its musical kazoo,
As shimmering asteroids dance in a queue.

Huddled in clusters, the odd ones meet,
Crafting unique galactic beats,
With laughter echoing through the dark,
A friendship forged with a quirky spark.

In this realm where boundaries blur,
The weirdos mingle, laughter will stir,
A cosmic carnival of joyful sounds,
Where happiness lies, and fun abounds.

Starlit Journeys Through Cosmic Seas

In a rocket made of cheese,
We sail on solar breeze,
With silly stars as guide,
And comets playing slide.

The moon forgot its hat,
And rolled down with a splat,
Jupiter sings a tune,
While Mars juggles the moon.

Venus dances in gold,
While Saturn's rings unfold,
A galactic clown parade,
In stardust masquerade.

We laugh as we collide,
In this cosmic joyride,
Through nebulae so bright,
On this starry night.

Secrets of the Solar Symphony

With trumpets made of light,
Planets groove through the night,
Uranus plays the drum,
While Mercury hums some.

The sun struts on the stage,
In a polka-dot rage,
While Pluto makes a jest,
In his small, offbeat quest.

The asteroids do the twist,
In an orbital mist,
Neptune sings low and sweet,
With a rhythm to beat.

As starlight fills the air,
We find magic to share,
In this symphonic swirl,
With a giggle and twirl.

The Ballet of Celestial Bodies

Planets take to the floor,
In a waltz evermore,
With meteors at play,
They twirl in a ballet.

Starry pirouettes high,
As the asteroids fly,
Mars steps to the beat,
In a cosmic retreat.

Moonbeams drape the night,
In a shimmering light,
While the sun leads the dance,
With a playful glance.

Around they spin and leap,
This is no time for sleep,
In the theater of space,
Where all wonders embrace.

Observing the Eclipses of Emotion

When the moon steals the show,
And emotions overflow,
We giggle through the dark,
As shadows leave their mark.

A solar wink from afar,
Makes the night feel bizarre,
Planets pair up with glee,
In a cosmic spree.

The stars laugh at our plight,
As we ponder the night,
With emotions in orbit,
In a playful puppet.

As eclipses come and fade,
We dance in this parade,
With grins wide and sincere,
In the night skies so clear.

The Parable of the Lost Pulsars

In a sky where time forgot,
Pulsars played hopscotch—forgotten but hot.
They blink in Morse, a cosmic game,
For those who seek fortune, not for fame.

One twinkled too hard, its light went astray,
Chasing a comet that shimmered like hay.
A cosmic mishap, or just a bad joke?
The pulsar giggled, leaving all folks broke.

With each quirky beat, it danced round and round,
While black holes chuckled, not making a sound.
A tale of the lost, a rhythm so sly,
In the vast unknown, they forever will fly.

Dreamscape of the Evaporated Stars

Once stars were bright, now they're puffs of delight,
Waltzing away in the soft moonlight.
They giggle and swirl, in a gassy ballet,
No gasping for air, just vapors at play.

One winked too loud, a puff of spun sugar,
While nearby comets all said, "What a booger!"
A runaway star, lost in a whim,
Floating away like a whimsical dream.

In the dreamscape they live, on laughter's soft breeze,
Creating a ruckus, whatever they please.
The universe chuckles at their trail of bright,
For funny encounters make skies feel just right.

The Riddle of Gravity's Tapestry

Gravity chuckled, a prankster in space,
Pulling at planets with a mischievous grace.
"Why do you spin?" the stars often moan,
As moons cling on tight, like a dog with a bone.

In the dance of the orbs, a riddle is spun,
Why is the black hole the ultimate fun?
"Drop in, take a ride, but bring your best snack!"
And galaxies giggled, while stars played a hack.

At the edge of the cosmos, a jest was laid bare,
Where spacetime can stretch and oddities flare.
With each little twist, gravity plays,
In a tapestry woven in whimsical ways.

Fragments of a Stellar Sunset

As the sun dips low, in a colorful gasp,
Fragments of stars in the cosmos clasp.
It's a cheeky bonfire, a cosmic soirée,
With nebulae swirling in a wild ballet.

Planets throw shade from their orbiting pods,
While comets wink slyly at the audience gods.
Each spark of light is a giggle aloud,
As the universe wraps in a whimsical shroud.

The last light of day is a winking delight,
As all of space revels in the playful night.
With laughter and joy that forever exists,
Fragments of twilight dance in cosmic twists.

The Sighs of Silent Nebulas

In the dark where gases play,
Whispers float and drift away.
Starry hiccups, cosmic sighs,
Giggling at the spinning skies.

Colors clash in pastel hues,
Nebulae dance in fanciful muse.
They twirl and twist like silly clowns,
Painting portraits of made-up towns.

Planets peek through smoky veils,
Telling tales of cosmic fails.
"Is that a comet? Oh, what a jest!"
Stars chuckle at the universe's fest.

Lost in laughter, they drift and tease,
Creating joy with cosmic ease.
In the sighs of the quiet night,
Every spark brings pure delight.

A Flutter Among the Celestial Gossamer

Wondrous wings of light float high,
Moths made of stardust flit and fly.
On gossamer threads they swing,
Whispering secrets of cosmic zing.

Asteroids dress in shiny wraps,
Glimmering like celestial naps.
Do they know they're just rocks in space?
They smile back, embracing their place.

Each twinkle a wink, a playful jest,
Galaxies spinning—what a quest!
They giggle through the vacuum wide,
In this cosmic carnival, they abide.

A flutter here, a flutter there,
Among planets with flair and care.
In the dance of the unseen spree,
Laughter echoes eternally.

Rhythms of the Astral Wanderlust

Stardust shuffles to a beat,
Planets groove with funky feet.
Jupiter laughs as it spins so fast,
While Saturn circles with its rings amassed.

Comets tailgate with brilliant flair,
Conductor of the solar air.
They're whimsically weaving through the sky,
While UFOs wave in passersby.

Synchronized in their dance of flight,
They twirl and twist in sheer delight.
"Want to join?" they ask the moon,
As stars clap along to the cosmic tune.

Echoes of giggles stir the void,
In this symphony, none deployed.
In the rhythms that never cease,
The universe finds its joyful peace.

Moonlit Promenade of Unseen Galaxies

Beneath the glow of lunar beams,
Galaxies waltz in joyous dreams.
Hidden in shadows, they come alive,
Chasing comets as they dive.

With each twirl, a starlet beams,
Swaying softly to silvery themes.
They stumble, they sway, a cosmic show,
With laughter that only the stars know.

The Milky Way joins in the fun,
Like a necklace spun from the sun.
Clusters giggle, swirling round,
In a moonlit ball where joy abounds.

Frisky sleigh rides of starlit cheer,
Across the vastness, they persevere.
As unseen galaxies prance and play,
The nightingale of space leads the way.

The Labyrinth of Floating Lights

In a maze of twinkling glow,
Bouncing balls of cosmic show,
Asteroids dress in shiny hats,
Dancing round like playful cats.

Nebulas stir in a poof of haze,
With starry confetti set to amaze,
Laughter echoes in the void,
As planets jive, most overjoyed.

Gravity's game is quite absurd,
With wobbly comets that swing and spurd,
Laughing moons in silly spins,
Join in for the cosmic wins!

So grab your rover, ride the tide,
In the stellar parade, take a wild slide!
For in this playground of the night,
Fun reigns supreme, a dazzling sight!

Makeup of the Mythical Moons

Jupiter's moon with glittering eyes,
Winks at Saturn, who wears a disguise,
With rings that sparkle like fancy bling,
They gossip and giggle, oh what fun they bring!

Uranus rolls with a quirky twist,
While Neptune dreams, lost in mist,
Each cycle they paint their faces bright,
Crafting masterpieces under starlit night.

A comet crashes the beauty bash,
With a rainbow tail and a sparkling splash,
They laugh and cheer in total delight,
The artwork of space, a joyous sight!

In this colorful cosmic guise,
The moons unite, in laughter they rise,
For every twinkle in the dark above,
Is a masterpiece born from celestial love!

Meditations on the Wandering Galaxies

Galaxies swirl in a playful chase,
Doing cartwheels in the boundless space,
Starry laughter spills and twirls,
As lightyears dance in cosmic swirls.

Orion hides behind a bright veil,
With a wink and a nod, he tells a tale,
Of space dust parties that last all night,
Where galaxies giggle, oh what a sight!

A black hole whispers with secrets untold,
But comets dash in, bold and uncontrolled,
Using starlight as silly confetti,
Creating a spectacle, bright and ready!

So when you gaze at the sky up above,
Know it's a playground, sprinkled with love,
For in this vast, absurd dance of glee,
The universe winks, 'Come join in, free!'

Fantasies of the Cosmic Companions

Aliens gather on a starlit spree,
With cosmic snacks and laughter, whee!
Spaceships twirl like oversized kites,
Painting the dark with silly lights.

Martians juggle planets with ease,
While Venus sings with a breeze,
In a gathering of cheerful friends,
Where the fun of stargazing never ends.

Cosmic rays sprinkle while they play,
Grinning comets zoom in, hooray!
With every laugh, a new world is born,
In the galaxy's joy, never a forlorn.

So let us dance among the stars,
With cosmic companions, oh what bizarre!
For in this universe vast and wide,
We find the laughter tucked inside!

The Enigma of the Shattered Ring

In a dance of bits and bits,
The ring spun past, with wobbles and fits.
It laughed at gravity's silly pull,
Like a child in a candy store, so full.

With chunks and chunks that twirled about,
Every piece had a curious shout.
"Why fit in when you can float?"
"Join us for a galactic boat!"

While some just rolled, others did fly,
A cosmic game of tag in the sky.
"Catch me if you can!" they all cried,
As they bounced off Saturn, with joy and pride.

Oh, the enigma of that shattered sight,
A playground for dust in the starlit night.
Each fragment a joke, set free to cheer,
In a quirky ring dance, they disappear.

Fantasia on the Edge of Time

Tick-tock went the cosmic clock,
As planets tickled a spacetime rock.
They pirouetted, they danced in glee,
In a time-warped ballet, so wild and free.

The sun grinned wide, in a fiery mood,
While comets joined, their tails a rude.
"Don't rush us, we're just having fun!"
They twirled around, like a hotdog bun.

Wormholes yawned and stretched their backs,
Like lazy cats on starlit tracks.
"Jump through me!" said one with a wink,
"But mind your head, give it a think!"

In this whirl of time and space,
They found the joy in their odd race.
With giggles echoing across the void,
A fanciful journey none would avoid.

Whirling Dervishes of the Cosmic Sea

In swirling waves of a stellar sea,
Dervishes danced just to be free.
They twirled past planets, swung 'round the sun,
"Join our waltz! It's cosmic fun!"

Galaxies swayed beneath their feet,
A dizzying rhythm, a celestial beat.
With arms outstretched and skirts a-fly,
They laughed at the stars, swirling high.

Each spin brought forth a comet's kiss,
In a cosmic whirl, who could resist?
"Catch me!" cried one with a gleeful shout,
While the others chased, roundabout.

In this whirlpool of light and cheer,
The joy of existence was perfectly clear.
Dervishes spun among the divine,
As laughter echoed through the cosmic line.

The Forgotten Orbs of Ancient Skies

In quiet corners of the midnight dome,
Forgotten orbs made their secret home.
Dusty pranks under galactic beds,
Whispering tales that space far spreads.

They played peek-a-boo with the stray stardust,
Tickling past moons, in a cosmic gust.
"Once we were kings!" they'd proudly boast,
As they chased a rogue asteroid, full of toast.

With smiles that glimmered like ancient suns,
They raced through the cosmos, oh what fun!
"We're still here, just lost in the flow!"
They giggled as they wandered, to and fro.

And though the universe forgets their names,
Their laughter echoes in celestial games.
For in the shadows where memories lie,
The orbs still twinkle, up in the sky.

Hymn to the Eclipsing Souls

When the moon wears shades, it's quite a sight,
Stars play hide and seek, all through the night.
Planets gossip in their cosmic dance,
Gravity takes a break; let's lose our pants!

Comets with tails, they twirl with glee,
Asteroids crash like they're on a spree.
In this dark void, we jest with fate,
As space-time laughs at our cosmic gait.

Rhapsody of the Cosmic Theatre

In the theatre of stars, the show's intense,
Asteroids throw popcorn with no recompense.
Martians applaud as the meteors dive,
Galaxies twinkle, they tend to connive.

Planets wear costumes, such flare and style,
Saturn's rings sparkle, oh what a pile!
Neptune's blue trumpet, a jazzy delight,
While Venus just sighs—why'd I wear white?

The Unseen Chronicles of the Galaxy

Black holes get hungry, it's really a shame,
They gobble up worlds without feeling the blame.
Neutrinos flip-flop like they're at the beach,
Light-speed is laughing, the cosmos is leech.

In this grand story that few dare to write,
A quasar's bursting at the heart of the night.
Wormholes play tricks, they knot time with ease,
While stardust giggles, this nonsense won't cease.

Reverie of the Celestial Nomads

Travelers of space with sandwiches in hand,
Flirting with gravity, it's all so unplanned.
Jupiter's storms toss our lunch to the void,
But who needs a meal when you're feeling buoyed?

Pluto's a loner; we send him a text,
'Join us for fun!'—it's always perplexed.
The moons hold a circus, bright lights in the night,
While space-time chuckles at their silly plight.

The Aesthetic of Cosmic Chaos

In a galaxy far, far away,
Stars wear hats and dance all day.
Planets chase after comets fast,
While the moons yell, "Don't fall, you'll crash!"

Black holes spin in a dizzying way,
Gobbling galaxies like a buffet play.
Supernovae throw a light show grand,
With aliens waving their greenish hands.

Asteroids play catch with each other,
Taking detours, oh what a bother!
Meteor showers raining down popcorn,
Wishing on snacks till the dawn is born.

Quasars zoom by with a quirky flair,
Whistling tunes through the cosmic air.
In this chaos, laughter prevails,
As the cosmos tells its funniest tales.

Whispers of the Astronomical Anomalies

Nebulas giggle in shades of bright,
While space whales swim in the starry night.
Wormholes twist like a funhouse maze,
Spitting out socks in a cosmic craze.

Aliens prank with their laser beams,
Drawing funny faces, or so it seems.
Time travel blunders make me spin,
Arriving late for the party's been.

Comets tease with their brilliant tails,
Making wishes that ride on cosmic gales.
Gravity's prank pulls us down to the ground,
As laughter echoes without making a sound.

Each quasar's a disco ball in disguise,
Reflecting the fun in the universe's eyes.
So let's toast to quirks and oddities,
In this cosmic dance of anomalies.

Visions of the Eternal Twilight

Twilight's dance glimmers with zany sights,
Where constellations chatter through starry nights.
Vampire stars wear capes made of light,
While comets giggle at their own flight.

A red giant grumbles, its time's almost here,
While little white dwarfs bring laughter and cheer.
In stellar lounge chairs, they sip cosmic tea,
Sharing tales of mischief, oh what glee!

Galactic twirls spin around like a top,
Where time takes a break and fun never stops.
Shooting stars race, but no one keeps score,
In this eternal twilight, who could want more?

With each passing light year, chuckles arise,
As the universe blinks with twinkling eyes.
So join the cosmic joke and rejoice,
In visions that tickle and make you voice!

Portraits of Celestial Peculiarities

Planets in bow ties strike a pose,
Grinning wide under the cosmic rose.
Mercury winks, while Jupiter laughs,
As Saturn shows off its ringed beautiful halves.

Pluto claims it's the cutest of all,
Even if it's short and a bit small.
Mars throws confetti, a red party treat,
While Venus does cartwheels on its own feet.

Sirius the dog star fetches the sun,
Chasing light beams, oh what fun!
Galaxies blossom like flowers in bloom,
Creating a spectacle, wiping out gloom.

So here's to the wonders that spark our delight,
With celestial quirks lighting up the night.
Each star holds a laugh, each moon has a tale,
In these portraits of oddities, we set sail.

The Musicality of Cosmic Wonders

In the sky where stars collide,
Planets dance with joy and pride.
Asteroids play a merry tune,
While comets waltz beneath the moon.

Saturn strums a ring-shaped harp,
Jupiter hums, a friendly lark.
Each twirl and twist a cosmic show,
Galaxies spin, oh what a glow!

Shooting stars like high notes fly,
While black holes suck in a sly sigh.
Nebulas puff in colorful bursts,
As supernovas quench their thirsts.

A cosmic band with glee and flair,
In the void, they float without a care.
Tune into space, where laughter gleams,
In this universe of silly dreams.

Duet of Dissonant Orbs

Two planets near, a quirky sight,
One's day is dark, the other bright.
They bicker over who's the best,
In their heated, stellar jest.

Moons laugh loud at their silly fight,
A trio joins—with glee, delight.
They spin and twirl, an odd parade,
In this vibrant cosmic charade.

A comet cuts in, all dressed in tail,
Adding flair to their swirling tale.
Uranus winks with a cheeky grin,
While Earth rolls eyes, 'where to begin?'

So here's to orbs, that laugh and play,
In the endless cosmos, bright as day.
Their playful tunes, a perfect blend,
A delightful dance that never ends.

The Ballet of the Belated Dawn

Dawn arrives on cosmic stage,
Unfolding light, an endless page.
Stars bow down, their dances done,
As the universe greets the sun.

Planets yawn with sleepy eyes,
While meteors race, an early rise.
The Milky Way in tutus sways,
In this ballet of bright displays.

Oh, the sun trips on its ray,
Stumbling through the Milky Way.
Asteroids giggle, a comic scene,
As they glide in a grand machine.

The day breaks forth with giggles bright,
A wobbly waltz of pure delight.
In this spectacle, all join in,
For the cosmic dance to spin and spin.

Observations from the Cosmic Overlook

From high above the velvet seas,
I watch the planets shift with ease.
Saturn's hat, a quirky find,
While Neptune stares, with eyes so kind.

Stars throw shade in playful glints,
While comets race and do their spins.
Black holes bubble with a silent laugh,
In this grand, celestial photograph.

Aliens wave from distant bars,
As UFOs zip past like shooting stars.
Jokes abound in the stellar realm,
With cosmic giggles at the helm.

So here I sit, a cosmic peep,
Where the universe seems to leap.
With laughter ringing through the void,
In this journey, joy is deployed.

Mysterious Moons of the Milky Way.

Round and round, they spin and twirl,
Bouncing around in a cosmic whirl.
With winks and nods, they tease the night,
Invisible friends in silver light.

Some wear masks, others sport hats,
A party of rocks, like cheeky cats.
They giggle and gleefully sing their tune,
Those mysterious moons, beneath the moon.

One plays hide and seek with the sun,
While another juggles comets for fun.
They swap silly tales of worlds far away,
Creating mischief in the Milky Way.

With craters and dust, they're quite the sight,
An oddball crew, a cosmic delight.
So let's raise a toast to the moonlit crew,
For in this galaxy, they outshine the blue!

Celestial Whispers of Forgotten Moons

Once upon a time, they drifted alone,
Forgotten by many, just dust and stone.
But whispers of laughter in silence throng,
Echoing softly, in cosmic song.

Lost in the shadows of brighter stars,
They played silly games on Jupiter's bars.
With popcorn clouds and asteroid pies,
Their humor transcends the darkest skies.

They scribbled their names on a comet's tail,
Eagerly sharing their interstellar tale.
For even in gloom, they know how to jest,
Unruly orbs, on a laugh-filled quest.

So turn up your ears to the sky's secrets,
For those moons still laugh, and it's truly epic.
Let's dance with these echoes, so quirky and bright,
In the grand theater of the starry night!

The Dance of Distant Planets

Planets in tutus twirl and sway,
Spinning around in a giggling ballet.
One trips on a star, another does the splits,
Whirling through galaxies, performing skits.

With rings that shimmer and belts of dust,
They move with flair that's a serious must.
Laughter erupts as Saturn drops low,
In a twinkling tumble, the laughter flows.

Neptune's doing the cha-cha with style,
While Venus winks and plays coy for a while.
Mars joins the fun, in a cosmic spree,
Sipping stardust in a frothy cup of glee.

So come take a seat, enjoy the show,
A raucous space dance, put on from below.
For in the vast dark, where silence may reign,
These dancing planets bring joy to the plane!

Echoes from a Stellar Circus

Step right up, see the cosmic feats,
A circus of wonders, where stardust meets.
Check out the rings, they twinkle and spin,
As the stellar clowns perform their wild din.

The sun juggles planets with whimsical flair,
While comets zip past in a dazzling glare.
Galaxies whirl like a cotton candy sky,
With nests of black holes that swish on by.

Mars leads a parade on a red, bouncy ball,
While Saturn's rings echo laughter for all.
"More popcorn!" the stars shout, giggling with glee,
While meteors streak through like a comet on spree.

So gather your friends and enjoy the night,
In this circus of wonders, all sparkly bright.
Where echoes of laughter paint cosmic scenes,
In a stellar carnival, full of sweet dreams!

www.ingramcontent.com/pod-product-compliance
Lightning Source LLC
Chambersburg PA
CBHW070749220426
43209CB00083B/196